Vergangenheitsbewältigung:
Germany's Holocaust Journey

Dominik Herzog

Abstract

This book methodically examines the decades-long process in which Germany has garnered its reputation as a model for confronting and reconciling with its dark history. Much of this has been attributed to the embodiment of *Vergangenheitsbewältigung* or, "the process of coming to terms with the past." Between 1933 and 1945, Nazi Germany and its collaborators perpetrated the deadliest genocide in world history, killing more than 6 million Jews and millions of other victims of marginalized groups. After the conclusion of World War II and the ultimate defeat of Nazi Germany, the country was physically devastated, and most Germans refused to even discuss the Holocaust. As successive generations of young Germans came of age, they began confrontations with their elders that would place Holocaust awareness at the forefront of academics, national politics, and everyday life. Furthermore, it led to unprecedented efforts to memorialize the victims of the Holocaust in meaningful ways, especially after the reunification of Germany. This thesis uses a secondary analysis of existing evidentiary sources to explore ways in which Germany has become a leader in confronting its genocidal past, focusing specifically on Holocaust awareness, memorialization, and the role of *Vergangenheitsbewältigung* in the process.

Table of Contents

Chapter I: Introduction 1

Chapter II: Methodology & Literature Review 6

Chapter III: Background – The Holocaust 9

Chapter IV: Findings 12

    4.1 Collective Memory and Guilt in Postwar Germany 12

    4.2 Emergence of *Vergangenheitsbewältigung* 17

    4.3 The Cold War, Moral Leadership & Reparations with Israel 18

    4.4 Holocaust Education & Anne Frank's Diary 21

    4.5 Seeking Justice: The Impacts of the Adolf Eichmann Trial 24

    4.6 The '68ers' and *Vergangenheitsbewältigung* 26

    4.7 The Media: Effects of NBC's *Holocaust* on
Vergangenheitsbewältigung 28

    4.8 Holocaust Memory Through Counter-Memorials 31

    4.9 Memorialization Following Reunification 33

Chapter V: Conclusion 40

Literature Cited 44

Appendix 49

Chapter I: Introduction

Between 1941 and 1945, Nazi Germany and its collaborators perpetrated the deadliest genocide in human history in its attempt to exterminate European Jews and other minority groups. By the time Germany surrendered to the Allies on May 7, 1945, the Nazi regime had murdered over 6 million Jews and millions of other non-Jewish victims, according to the Illinois Holocaust Museum and Education Center (2023). However, unlike other nations which have perpetrated genocide and mass murder, Germany has taken a leading position in recognizing its perpetration of the Holocaust and making efforts to ensure the world never forgets. A. Dirk Moses (2007) supports this argument, writing, "In the eyes of many, the West German and, since 1990, the united German experiences have exemplified how posttotalitarian and postgenocidal societies "come to terms with the past" (Moses, 2007, p. 46).

In the years since its defeat in World War II, Germany has recognized its culpability in perpetrating the Holocaust. However, this process of remembering and memorializing was not immediate, as the trauma of the war and immediate needs of survival took precedence over remembering. It would take years until systematic memory was initiated following the war, but the process ultimately drove *Vergangenheitsbewältigung* forward. It is also important to note for context, that Holocaust memory and memorialization was very different in East and West Germany after division. This thesis will focus on the process in West Germany prior to the reunification of Germany.

Through museums, monuments and other forms of memorialization, the nation has embraced its responsibility for the Holocaust, and has made progress throughout the years in an effort to never forget the victims. The purpose of these memorials throughout modern Germany are a major reason why the nation is viewed by many around the world as a remarkable example of a nation and its people overcoming their dark past and making efforts to reconcile the atrocities committed. According to Kirsten Harjes (2022):

> …these memorials generally attempt to fulfill three functions: to mourn and commemorate the dead, to educate their audiences, and to politically and socially represent contemporary German citizens…Not only does German history appear very different to Germans of different generations but for most members of minority groups in Germany today, the Holocaust does not seem to be part of a history shared with their ethnic German neighbors…immigrants from Turkey, the former Yugoslavia, or the former Soviet Union bring their own, often silent memories of racism and genocide. And yet, however difficult, the task of integrating these and other heritage communities into collective memory practices is vital (Harjes, 2022, pp. 139-140).

In order to fully understand why Germany is viewed as a world leader in confronting their dark history, the concept of collective memory must be discussed and applied to the overall process the nation has taken since the end of World War II.

The concept of collective memory is of critical importance when examining how Germany became a leader in recognizing and remembering its role in perpetrating the Holocaust. The framework of collective memory was first pioneered by French sociologist and philosopher Maurice Halbwachs (1992) prior to his death in 1945 and has been an important concept in historiography since. In his groundbreaking work, he argues that the memories of an individual are intrinsically linked to the overall memory of the collective:

> To be sure, everyone has a capacity for memory that is unlike that of anyone else…But individual memory is nevertheless a part or an aspect of group memory, since each impression and each fact…leaves a lasting memory…that is connected with the thoughts that come to us from the social milieu. One cannot in fact think about the events of one's past without discoursing upon them. But to discourse upon something means to connect within a single system of ideas…In

> this way, the framework of collective memory confines and binds our most intimate remembrances to each other… (Halbwachs, 1992, p. 53)

This individual connection to the collective becomes apparent when examining the role that memory has played in memorializing the Holocaust in the decades following World War II.

In recent years, Michael Rothberg (2009) has analyzed the role of multidirectional memory, specifically focusing on Germany and Holocaust memory as it relates to decolonization. He argues that by elevating the memory of a major event, in this case the Holocaust, it creates a multidirectional dynamic where violent histories converge in confrontation with each other, creating further complexities. Rothberg (2009) argues that Holocaust memory is a perfect example of the confrontation of violent histories:

> …far from blocking other historical memories from view in a competitive struggle for recognition, the emergence of Holocaust memory on a global scale has contributed to the articulation of other histories…The period between 1945 and 1962 contains both the rise of consciousness of the Holocaust as an unprecedented form of modern genocide and the coming to national consciousness and political independence of many of the subjects of European colonialism (Rothberg, 2009, pp. 6-7).

Collective and multidirectional memory are both crucial for reconnecting with the past, or in the case of Germany, working through it. Regardless of the application, collective memory shapes the connection and relationship groups often have with the past. The application of multidirectional memory also has created an environment where comparisons have been drawn between the Holocaust and other acts of extreme violence throughout history, bringing attention to other forms of genocide and extreme violence perpetrated against groups before and after the Holocaust. It also draws a critical link to the importance and centrality of collective memory when working through the past.

Historian Amos Funkenstein (1989) also argues the importance of collective memory within history:

> We naturally ascribe historical "consciousness" and "memory" to human collectives - family and tribe, nation and state. Nations are meant to remember their heroes "forever"; to perpetuate the memory of a person means to embed it in the collective memory, which forgets only failures and sins (Funkenstein, 1989 pp. 5-6).

What happens when, contrary to Funkenstein's assertion, the collective memory of a group does not forget, and instead takes concrete steps to ensure that the 'failures' and 'sins' are not forgotten? Germany's post-World War II history, multi-generational social movements, and examples of Holocaust memorialization serve as evidence of this, specifically through the embracement of *Vergangenheitsbewältigung*. The Collins German to English Dictionary defines *Vergangenheitsbewältigung* as the "process of coming to terms with the past" (Collins German-English Dictionary, 2023).

Germany, both when divided and later reunified, offers a unique case study to analyze critical questions through collective memory:

- How can a nation of perpetrators recognize and memorialize the victims of their actions?
- What factors have contributed to Germany taking a global lead in terms of recognition and reconciliation?
- What did Germany do specifically to create a culture of remembrance?
- Can a concept, such as *Vergangenheitsbewältigung,* be an effective catalyst that spurs memorialization and reconciliation across subsequent generations?

What is known is that Germany has taken a global stance on genocide prevention and Holocaust memorialization through its recognition of the collective, multi-generational guilt of German society, and has worked to ensure that future generations will never forget.

Chapter II: Methodology & Literature Review

The purpose of this thesis is to conduct an analysis of existing research and discuss the process in which Germany has come to embrace the concept of *Vergangenheitsbewältigung* and recognize its perpetration of the Holocaust. To successfully fulfill this purpose, I will conduct a secondary analysis of existing evidentiary research and bibliographic references. This thesis will examine various historical patterns from postwar to contemporary Germany. For this thesis, research and analysis will focus on West Germany during the years prior to reunification.

There are several important concepts and terms that are of critical importance to the research and analysis presented in this thesis that must be defined prior to additional discussion. Merriam-Webster defines memorialize in two different ways: "a) to address or petition by a memorial; b) to commemorate" (Merriam-Webster, 2023). It also defines memory in several different ways:

> a) the power or process of reproducing or recalling what has been learned and retained especially through associative mechanisms; b) the store of things learned and retained from an organism's activity or experience as evidenced by modification of structure or behavior or by recall and recognition; c) commemorative remembrance; d) the time within which past events can be or are remembered (Merriam-Webster, 2023)

Finally, it defines responsibility as: "1) the quality or state of being responsible: such as…moral, legal, or mental accountability (Merriam-Webster, 2023).

While Holocaust and Genocide Studies is a relatively new area of academia, there is ample existing scholarly research that focuses on Germany's memorialization of the Holocaust. Of the existing scholarly research, there are several key sources that have contributed to my research. Caroline Sharples' (2016) book *Postwar Germany and the Holocaust* provided ample evidence that helped to develop various patterns of Holocaust memory and memorialization from the end of World War II until the present. Historian Amos Funkenstein's (1989) article *Collective Memory and Historical Consciousness* proved to be an invaluable source. The roles of both collective memory and historical consciousness are important contributors that have led to Germany's present level of memorialization and embodiment of *Vergangenheitsbewältigung*. The works of Maurice Halbwachs (1992) and Michael Rothberg (2009) were crucial to exploring collective and multidirectional memory. These concepts are crucial to understanding the relationship that exists between working through the past and understanding the experiences of the collective. Daniel Levy and Jeffrey Olick (1997) also provide a strong analysis of the role of collective memory and its effect on both the identity of ordinary German citizens and the nation's political arena.

Wulf Kansteiner's (1999) research and analysis on the effect of *Vergangenheitsbewältigung* and how it has become incorporated into modern Germany over time proved to be an extremely helpful resource for researching this topic. Brian Ladd (1997), Martin Winstone (2010), Kirsten Harjes (2005), and Clint Smith (2022) all provided extremely valuable research on specific examples of Holocaust memorials in Germany, as well as excellent analysis of the meanings conveyed by them as it relates to *Vergangenheitsbewältigung*. A. Dirk Moses' (2021) article *The German Catechism* was unique in its analysis of *Vergangenheitsbewältigung*. While Moses (2021) discusses the process that has taken the nation so far from its Nazi past, he argues that Germany has not experienced the same success when confronting contemporary issues, including responses to the migrant crisis in the mid-2010s. This critical perspective was valuable, and emphasized the fact that this process has not been perfect or without flaws. While research for this thesis comes from a variety of sources, these proved to be some of the strongest for developing this secondary analysis. Each source provided important insight and information on the process in which Germany has earned its reputation through recognition and reconciliation as it relates to *Vergangenheitsbewältigung*.

Chapter III: Background - The Holocaust

At 11:11 AM on November 11, 1918, World War I came to an end. The German Empire had been decisively defeated on the battlefield. The Treaty of Versailles subsequently disarmed Germany and blamed the nation for the unprecedented horrors of World War I. It forced territorial concessions to be made and mandated reparations payments, significantly weakening the economy of the Weimar Republic, the successor state to the German Empire. Antisemitism also ran rampant in the Weimar Republic following World War I. Laurence Rees (2017) argues that this antisemitic environment caused much of the blame to fall on German Jews for the nation's defeat:

> The Jews…were also blamed for the loss of the war; the destruction of the old political regime based on the Kaiser; agreeing to the terms of the hated Versailles peace treaty; and participating in the Weimar government, which presided over the hyperinflation of the early 1920s (Rees, 2017, p. 12).

Rees (2017) further argues that this antisemitic blame provided an environment that led to the emergence of the Nazi party. During the 1920s, Adolf Hitler became a key figure in the Nazi party. Hitler made many vitriolic and antisemitic speeches to supporters that utilized widespread discontent to place all blame for defeat in World War I on German Jews. Hitler would continue this ideological hatred through the 1920s and into the 1930s.

In 1933, the Nazi Party became the largest political party in the Reichstag. Hitler was subsequently appointed Chancellor of Germany by President Paul von Hindenburg. As Hitler began to consolidate power, he used the 1933 fire at the Reichstag to justify emergency powers that would leave no check to his power, laying the foundation of Nazi Germany and marking the end of the Weimar Republic.

Now that a de facto dictatorship had been established, antisemitic violence and propaganda became even more widespread throughout Germany. Jews within Germany were increasingly targeted by the Nazi regime and found themselves vilified and ostracized from society as a result of state policies. The passage of the Nuremberg Laws in 1935 stripped German Jews of their citizenship and further curtailed what little remaining rights they still possessed. Pogroms against Jews were incited by the Nazi regime, culminating in *Kristallnacht* during 1938. Open violence against Jews had now become much more frequent and organized.

On September 1, 1939, the course of history was forever changed when Nazi Germany invaded Poland to begin World War II. As Germany quickly occupied more and more territory, Jews in Warsaw and other major cities were ghettoized by the Nazi occupiers in horrific conditions. Concentration camp systems began to be implemented in the captured territories in eastern Europe. Though camps, such as Dachau, had been established within Germany as early as the mid-1930s, they were used primarily for holding political prisoners and others who opposed the Nazi rise to power. By 1942, the participants of the infamous Wannsee Conference had determined that the current methods of killing, primarily shooting victims, was not efficient enough. As a result, Nazi concentration camps became sites that either served specific purposes to the regime through forced labor or became places of extermination and murder at rates never before seen. According to the Illinois Holocaust Museum and Education Center (2023), by mid-March of 1942, approximately 20-25% of all Jews killed during the Holocaust had already been murdered (2023). By 1943, the mass murder of Jews and other victims had been fully implemented, with the ultimate end goals of the Holocaust clearly identified by the Nazis. Both by bullet and by gas, the extermination continued until Nazi Germany was on the brink of defeat by the Allies. According to the Illinois Holocaust Museum and

Education Center (2023), camps with gas chamber facilities, among them, Auschwitz-Birkenau, Belzec, Chelmno, Majdanek-Lublin, Sobibor, and Treblinka, were the sites of murder for approximately 2,700,000 Jews and other victims (2023). By the time the Holocaust concluded at the end of World War II, Nazi Germany and its collaborators had systematically murdered over 6 million Jews and millions of other victims. As A. Dirk Moses asserts in his article *The German Catechism*, the Holocaust is unique compared to other historical examples of genocide, as it was the first time a state had attempted to destroy a people solely based on ideology for the sake of complete extermination (Moses, 2021).

Chapter IV: Findings

4.1 Collective Memory and Guilt in Postwar Germany

On April 30, 1945, Adolf Hitler committed suicide as the Soviet Army was on the cusp of defeating the remains of the Nazi defense of Berlin. Eight days later, Allied forces accepted the unconditional surrender of Nazi Germany, ending the European theater of World War II. Germany lay in ruins and would remain territorially divided among different Allied zones of occupation. Entire cities and important infrastructure targets throughout Germany were razed in Allied bombing raids and remained critically damaged immediately after the war, leaving tens of millions homeless or displaced. During this time, the immediate priorities were finding food, water, and shelter for survival, not discussing or examining responsibility for the Holocaust.

Extermination and forced labor camps, as well as other evidence of the scale of atrocities perpetrated by Nazi Germany, were soon discovered by Soviet, American, British, and other Allied forces. German citizens under Allied occupation were forcibly confronted with accusations of collective responsibility for the Holocaust. During the initial occupation of Germany, a method widely used by Allied occupation troops throughout the country was forcing local residents near concentration camps and other sites of mass killings to bury or rebury both Jewish and non-Jewish victims of Nazi atrocities. Caroline Colls (2016) describes the forcible confrontations of German citizens:

> …the liberators were faced with thousands of bodies that had not been buried by the perpetrators and, as such, they were faced with the huge task of burying them…it was common practice for perpetrators, people deemed to have an association with the Third Reich and local communities to be forced to bury the corpses. This took place at Dachau, Buchenwald, Nordhausen, and Namering, and local people were forced to view the corpses, which were laid out in the camp grounds at the request of the American liberating forces (Colls, 2016, p.166)

The various Allied methods of forced concentration that were imposed after World War II effectively assigned collective guilt and responsibility on all German citizens. Christopher Mauriello (2017) describes the resulting guilt assigned to German civilians through forced exhumations and reburials after the war:

> In April and May 1945, American collective guilt was not a discursive device or an abstraction. Military field commanders and MG detachments directly accused Germans of collective guilt and carried out the sentence…through the politics of dead bodies. The dead bodies of concentration camp victims…discovered in multiple mass graves…became the site for American political claims of collective guilt of all Germans for the Nazi regime. The corpses became representative of all the innocent victims of Nazism…The exhumation, witnessing and reburial of the corpses by German townspeople were the punishments for all Germans regardless of their individual actions (Mauriello, 2017, pp. 181-182).

By assigning collective guilt to all German citizens, feelings of resentment towards Allied troops began to grow. This gave rise to alternative narratives and sense of escapism that aimed to disassociate Germans from the Nazi regime and therefore, from responsibility for perpetrating the Holocaust.

As a result of these instances of forced confrontation immediately after the war, German citizens were essentially forced to bear the full brunt of collective and moral responsibility. Jeffrey Olick (2003) draws a critical link between German citizens throughout the war who might be perceived as 'bystanders' and the concept of *Kollektivschuld* (collective guilt) introduced by Swiss psychoanalyst Carl Jung:

> In February of 1945, Jung gave an interview to a Zurich newspaper in which he stated that "the popular sentimental distinction between Nazis and opponents of the regime" was psychologically illegitimate. In an essay published shortly thereafter meant to clarify his inflammatory statements, Jung argued that all Germans were either actively or passively, consciously or unconsciously, participants in the atrocities, that the "collective guilt" of the Germans was "for psychologists a fact, and it will be one of the most important tasks of therapy to bring the Germans to recognize this guilt" (Olick, 2003, p. 110)

How was it plausible for Jung to assign collective guilt and responsibility upon all Germans, when opponents of the Nazi regime within Germany existed at severe risk to their lives? Olick (2003) continued to discuss and analyze Jung's argument, providing some clarification:

> Central to Jung's argument was his distinction between psychological guilt and moral or criminal guilt…There was a difference, he argued, between objective and subjective guilt: "Guilt," he insisted, "can be restricted to the lawbreaker only from the legal, moral, and intellectual point of view, but as a psychic phenomenon it spreads itself over the whole neighborhood. A house, a family, even a village where a murder has been committed," Jung argued, "feels the psychological guilt and is made to feel it by the outside world." His point is to understand the ways in which one can feel badly for an act that one has not in fact committed…Collective guilt, Jung thus argued, is… "a very real fact" (Olick, 2003, p. 110).

Jung's introduction of *Kollektivschuld* was controversial, but the concept itself is apparent when examining this immediate postwar period. The Allied occupation troops forced German citizens to confront and bear *Kollektivschuld* through the forced reburial of victims, the screening of atrocity films, and various other methods. Through these policies and actions, the frameworks of collective guilt and awareness of Nazi atrocities were now extended beyond only active participants. *Kollektivschuld* was now a collective guilt extended upon the citizens of Germany, who Jung asserts were both unconscious and passive participants.

The physical devastation caused by the war, coupled with initial Allied assumptions and policies, created many feelings among German civilians, including relief the war had ended, fear of an unsure future, shame and grief. Whether they were active or passive participants, German civilians were forced to both confront the traumatic reality that their nation had perpetrated the atrocities of the Holocaust, though not all accepted this notion. During the occupation, Allied troops often blamed responsibility for both

World War II and the Holocaust on all Germans, regardless of their actual roles during the conflict. These accusations created an environment characterized by the heavy guilt of *Kollektivschuld,* which in turn caused an increasing number of Germans to accept that their nation had perpetrated the Holocaust for the first time. This would begin the long process of working to come to terms with the nation's Nazi past.

While the roots of accepting their nation's role in perpetrating the Holocaust began to gain some traction, it is important to note that many Germans simply wanted to move on from the Third Reich and the war. The trauma of attempting to rebuild a destroyed nation, coupled with resentment toward Allied policies of forced confrontation, created a feeling that the Nazi regime and the war could be separated from German normal history, thereby forgetting rather than remembering. This significant obstacle would need to be overcome in the coming years to determine how and to what level Germany would remember the Holocaust in the future.

Despite the initial stages of coping and accepting responsibility, Harold Marcuse (2010) asserts that many early efforts to memorialize the Holocaust occurred outside of Germany during the immediate postwar years (Marcuse, 2010, p. 54). These earliest memorialization efforts were often led by the victims themselves, and usually commemorated specific sites or concentration camps in which atrocities were committed. While there were small portions of the German population that recognized the nation's responsibility for the Holocaust during this time, it was the extreme physical destruction of the nation and the grief of the defeated and occupied population that took immediate hold among the majority. Despite this, some Germans began to collectively develop feelings of guilt and responsibility for their nation's perpetration of the Holocaust, often through social and religious groups initially. During the immediate postwar period, these groups seemed to represent an outlier among Germans as a whole. However, there was pressure from the international community, led by the United States and the newly formed Israel, to acknowledge the Nazi past and make some effort to reconcile. There was also intense pressure by Western Jewish non-governmental organizations, such as the Jewish Committee for Relief Abroad, the American Jewish Joint Distribution Committee among others in urging Germany to acknowledge responsibility for the Holocaust and to seek compensation for the victims (Sharples, 2016, p. 57).

Despite the pressure, there were still large swaths of German society that felt that they were not directly to blame and therefore, felt that they should not have been included in this collective guilt. Jeffrey Olick and Daniel Levy (1997) concur that there were various social and environmental factors, including methods utilized by the Allied occupation forces, that led to this rejection of guilt:

> In the late 1940s and early 1950s, the emerging Federal Republic of Germany encountered many serious problems deriving from the Nazi past. In addition to the pervasive physical devastation, Germans faced a moral crisis of perhaps unprecedented proportions. Allied occupation forces confronted the defeated and destroyed German populace with the crimes it had supported, in settings including early forced tours of concentration camps, "reeducation" propaganda, and the trials of leading political and military figures at Nuremberg. All Germans in the Western zones of occupation who had been of legal age during the Nazi period were required to fill out questionnaires that were used as the basis for "denazificaion" proceedings (Olick & Levy, 1997, p. 925).

The questionnaires referenced by Olick and Levy (1997), revealed a troubling rift that emerged after Germans experienced this collective moral crisis. While some genuinely felt a sense of responsibility and shame, others were quick to compare the actions of Germany to other nations that committed mass atrocities during the war, asserting that they should also feel guilt and bear responsibility. This was highly problematic and ultimately led to alternative narratives. Many also tried to suppress the feeling of collective guilt by separating their postwar German nation from the Third Reich, the regime in power during the Holocaust and World War II. Others still, as Jung asserted, felt little responsibility because they believed they were passive bystanders.

Whatever justification these groups in German society used in an attempt to evade responsibility or separate themselves from the Holocaust could have ultimately become the path that Germany as a whole took. Over time, through the efforts of political, religious or grassroots movements and organizations, *Kollektivschuld* slowly began to gain traction and legitimacy in German society. As these efforts persisted, they would prove to be a critical part in the process that ultimately led to Germany recognizing responsibility for the Holocaust and acknowledging guilt. Beyond the external international pressures, one of the leading efforts that drove Germany to begin recognizing its responsibility for the Holocaust would be driven by successive generations of young Germans in the coming decades.

4.2 Emergence of *Vergangenheitsbewältigung*

As Germany lay in ruins following the conclusion of World War II, feelings of guilt and responsibility diverged at a critical juncture within the identity of German collective memory. The immediate postwar years were marred by clear signs of historical amnesia among most Germans. This can be attributed to a variety of external and environmental factors, including the immediate need to rebuild the destroyed country, the onset of the Cold War and the resulting division of Germany. The beliefs of many Germans who felt they were not direct participants in perpetrating the Holocaust were also widespread, and many felt they bore no direct responsibility. A postwar poll cited by Morris Janowitz (1946) reveals the lack of perceived guilt and responsibility at the time:

> The main problem of the investigation was to supply the answers to such questions as "Under what circumstances did the German people believe that atrocities were committed?" "Who is believed to have committed them?" "Who is to be held responsible, and how, in their opinion, can it be prevented from occurring again?" …of the seventy German civilians…only three ascribed some element of guilt to the German people as a whole (Janowitz, 1946, pp. 143-144).

Despite the initial conflicting narratives, feelings, and debate, an emergence of individuals and organizations who felt Germans were collectively responsible began to increase in numbers. These individuals and groups came to embody and identify with the importance of the concept of *Vergangenheitsbewältigung,* or "overcoming the past."

After the initial postwar years, in which rebuilding a destroyed nation and addressing widespread guilt and trauma were paramount, Holocaust memory slowly became more important in West Germany, thanks in part to the growing focus on *Vergangenheitsbewältigung. Vergangenheitsbewältigung* represented a collective characterization of Germans who witnessed and survived the war, but now struggled to work through their experiences. In the coming years, it would become a central concept to the younger generation of Germans who were born after World War II and came of age in the 1960s. This younger generation of Germans would work to further elevate Holocaust awareness and understanding as part of the larger student protest movement that began in 1968 after the attempted assassination of Rudi Dutschke, a key leader and spokesman (Merritt, 1969, p. 516).

4.3 The Cold War, Moral Leadership & Reparations with Israel

Following the Yalta Conference in 1945, the former Third Reich was divided into Soviet, American, British, and later French occupation zones. By 1949, the country was officially divided as a result of the Cold War geopolitical dynamic that pitted a western-oriented Federal Republic of Germany (West Germany) against a Soviet satellite state known as the German Democratic Republic (East Germany).

Beyond the initial focus of rebuilding the nation, West Germany was also economically ravaged as a result of the war. Seeking economic growth and sustainability, Chancellor Konrad Adenauer recognized that it was necessary for postwar West Germany to reintegrate with the international community, many of whom were former enemies. Jewish organizations within West Germany and other Western nations began numerous efforts to urge Adenauer's government to enter some form of reparations agreement with the newly established State of Israel. The West German and Israeli governments began negotiations at the end of 1951 (Sharples, 2016). In a solemn speech to the Bundestag, Chancellor Adenauer, on behalf of West Germany and its citizens, publicly recognized and decried the horrors and suffering inflicted upon Jews in Nazi occupied areas during World War II. Chancellor Adenauer also explicitly referenced restitution to Jewish victims and citizens who had their property either seized or destroyed by Nazi Germany (Sharples, 2016).

Adenauer's calls for reparations to Israel and his subsequent speech to the Bundestag were both highly controversial within the West German government. Opponents criticized Chancellor Adenauer for his stance on reparations, questioning not only the lack of cohesive agreement in the Bundestag, but also whether West Germany could actually pay while facing severe debt. In addition to a divided government, there was also significant opposition by citizens of West Germany. Carole Fink (2007) cites the results of a 1952 West German public opinion poll which, "...revealed that only 11 percent of the population unqualifiedly endorsed the agreement, 44 percent considered it "superfluous," 24 percent agreed…and 21 percent were undecided (Fink, 2007, 277).

Despite the fierce controversies, West Germany and Israel officially signed a reparations agreement in September 1952, known as the Luxembourg Agreement. Sharples (2016) argues that this agreement was an example of the West German government enacting policy that recognized Germany's responsibility the atrocities committed during the Holocaust by the Nazi regime, and represented a meaningful step towards reconciliation:

> This was a historic occasion…the signing of the Luxembourg Agreement on 10 September 1952…pledged DM3b to Israel, and DM450m to the Conference on Jewish Material Claims against Germany, an organization that represented Jews living outside of Israel. This reparations treaty recognized Jews' fundamental right to compensation and secured the FRG's responsibility for providing this (Sharples, 2016, p. 60).

The reparations agreement between West Germany and Israel was a significant step forward in the country's efforts to acknowledge responsibility and represented *Vergangenheitsbewältigung* through government policy.

In the face of fierce controversy and division that resulted from his decision, Chancellor Adenauer's role in beginning negotiations with Israel should be recognized as a true embodiment of strong moral leadership. J. Patrick Dobel (1998) discusses several characteristics that are critical to a strong moral leader, and many can be applied to Adenauer during this time:

> Responsible political leaders should exercise judgment that unites moral and practical concerns…A leader's virtues define the stable cognitive and emotional responses to…guide, inform, and sustain judgment and action. This involves…a trained perception where an individual identifies the morally salient aspects of a situation and frames judgment around these aspects… (Dobel, 1998, p. 75).

While the decision was initially unpopular among West German citizens and members of the Bundestag, Adenauer demonstrated moral leadership by continuing to negotiate. He believed that the agreement to pay reparations to Israel was not only a step toward reconciliation, but was also an obligation of the Bonn Government. Carl Anthon (1963) also argues that Chancellor Adenauer's moral leadership was critical in acknowledging both the importance of *Vergangenheitsbewältigung* and the feeling of German responsibility for the Holocaust:

> Signs of possible recrudescence of anti-Semitism and neo-Nazism have produced vigorous reactions from official and unofficial quarters. It should be remembered…that Adenauer himself has consistently taken the lead in promoting legislative measures to reconcile and compensate Jews (as far as this is possible) at home and abroad (Anthon, 1963, p. 200).

Through his moral leadership as West Germany's first Chancellor, Adenauer's decision to come to an agreement with Israel demonstrated that *Vergangenheitsbewältigung* was gaining traction. Ultimately, the reparations debate brought grappling with Germany's perpetration of the Holocaust to the forefront, which was almost unthinkable during the initial postwar years prior.

4.4 Holocaust Education & Anne Frank's Diary

For the next generation that either could not remember World War II or were born after its conclusion, Germany's perpetration of the Holocaust became a major focal point in confronting the Nazi past. While uniform Holocaust educational standards and historiography were still years away from being developed, West Germany did insert limited frameworks relative to Holocaust history, memory, and responsibility. Although early Holocaust education in West Germany was limited by a variety of external factors, chiefly the political climate of the Cold War, Caroline Sharples (2016) argues that simply the presence of this curriculum in the classroom had major impacts on how younger generations would confront German responsibility for perpetrating the Holocaust:

> ...by 1949, there were at least six examples of Nazi crimes that could be discussed in schools...The extent to which these themes were addressed in the classroom, and the way in which they were interpreted, though, would be affected by both Cold War politics and teachers' own ability to talk about the past... (Sharples, 2016, p. 150).

Establishing these early educational frameworks for students was a critical development in bringing Holocaust awareness to a more elevated position in West Germany. While this was a significant step forward in the process of *Vergangenheitsbewältigung*, Stephen Pagaard (1995) argues that there were a multitude of problems with the curriculum, specifically regarding student textbooks, which led to criticism:

> Textbooks in the 1950s in the Federal Republic were characterized...by their general neglect of the Holocaust and by a tendency to absolve the German people as a whole of responsibility, a feat usually accomplished by focusing on the Nazi terror state. Other characteristics of these texts were their willingness to free the Wehrmacht of responsibility, the relative juxtaposition of contemporary Russian crimes, and the citation of sources only from the vantage point of the perpetrators...By the late 1960s more balanced coverage of the Nazi genocide began to gradually appear (Pagaard, 1995, p. 548).

While it is necessary to acknowledge the problems and criticisms of the initial frameworks implemented in West Germany, further refinement created a more historically accurate depiction of the nation's responsibility for perpetrating the Holocaust.

Arguably one of the most important moments leading to increased Holocaust awareness occurred in the mid-1950s and thrust West Germany into a nationwide reckoning and debate. Anne Frank's *The Diary of a Young Girl* was translated into German, and it quickly became the best-selling paperback book in the history of West Germany (Marcuse, 1998, p.422). This widespread exposure of a victim's real experiences was an important catalyst in moving West Germany away from shunning its responsibility for the Holocaust. Now, *The Diary of a Young Girl* brought these difficult topics and conversations to the forefront. Alex Sagan (1995) asserts that the publishing of Anne Frank's diary, coupled with its historic popularity in West Germany, were critical to elevating Holocaust memory for the postwar generation and further demonstrated that *Vergangenheitsbewältigung* was gaining traction:

> In…Germany…Anne Frank's story attained fame during years of relative silence about the Holocaust, years in which resistance to open discussion of the topic was the norm…contact with Anne's story brought millions of Germans…closer to grasping the injustice of the Nazi persecution and the suffering of European Jews (Sagan, 1995, pp. 95-96).

The Diary of a Young Girl's undeniable popularity spurred a collective self-reckoning experienced by much of West German society as they continued to work through coming to terms with the Nazi past.

Anne Frank's diary was crucial in eliminating the strong reluctance of discussing the Holocaust throughout West Germany. At around the same time Holocaust education was implemented in schools, the West German government actively attempted to distance itself from the Nazi regime while reintegrating with the West. Despite these efforts, the first West German government under Chancellor Konrad Adenauer contained many ex-Nazis and individuals who were heavily involved with National Socialism prior to the end of World War II. Harold Marcuse (1998) argues that since West Germans were beginning to examine their recent dark past through the process of *Vergangenheitsbewältigung*, the very idea of former Nazis in the Bonn Government spurred outrage and brought the Holocaust to the forefront once again:

> Between Christmas 1959 and the end of January 1960, a wave of anti-Semitic vandalism, partially supported by East German agitators, tarnished Bonn's

carefully established distancing from the Nazi past. The vandalism prompted official investigations of history textbooks and curricula, the publication of new textbooks, and increased pedagogical attention to the process of "mastering the past" (*Bewältigung der Vergangenheit*) ...Revelations about officials' ties with the Nazis, once brushed aside as East German subversion, now elicited formal responses and explanations (Marcuse, 1998, pp. 423-424).

These criticisms of the Adenauer government serve as strong examples of the increasing effects *Vergangenheitsbewältigung* now had among citizens of West Germany. The revelations of ex-Nazis serving in Adenauer's government created uproar that shattered the silence and signaled a reversal of the previous hesitance to discuss the Holocaust. Now, West Germans were not afraid to look at themselves and their nation in a critical manner, further embracing the sense of collective responsibility for the perpetration of the Holocaust. Thus, the concept of *Vergangenheitsbewältigung* had sparked a major step forward in attempting to overcome the Nazi past. This process would be amplified even more by the younger, postwar generation of Germans who had now come of age and would later be known as the '68ers.'

4.5 Seeking Justice: The Impacts of the Adolf Eichmann Trial

Another important event that significantly heightened Holocaust awareness among West Germans was the 1961 trial of Adolf Eichmann. Eichmann initially escaped Allied custody and fled to Argentina, where he was later located and captured by the Israeli Security Services. Following his capture, he was brought to Jerusalem to stand trial (United States Holocaust Memorial Museum, 2018). The United States Holocaust Memorial Museum (2018) discusses Eichmann's high-ranking status within the Nazi Party as well as his role in the Holocaust:

> Adolf Eichmann was one of the most pivotal actors in the implementation of the "Final Solution." Charged with managing and facilitating the mass deportation of Jews to ghettos and killing centers in the German-occupied East, he was among

the major organizers of the Holocaust (United States Holocaust Memorial Museum, 2018).

Due to his high-ranking position during the war and the significant role he played in planning at the Wannsee Conference in 1942, Eichmann's trial quickly gained international attention. In West Germany, the trial was watched closely, indicative of unprecedented interest in the Holocaust among the masses. Caroline Sharples (2016) argues that the 1961 Eichmann Trial also resulted in a stronger connection to *Vergangenheitsbewältigung* among West Germans:

> While accounts have paid some attention to the pedagogic impact of war crimes proceedings, the trials' effect on Vergangenheitsbewältigung has often been assumed, rather than probed in any great depth…there has been growing interest between justice and the formation of historical memory, with a number of scholars exploring the extent to which war crimes trials were able to effect a more critical public understanding of the Holocaust. We have already seen that events such as the Eichmann or Auschwitz trials of the 1960s have often been advanced as key turning points in effecting greater West German discussion of the past… (Sharples, 2016, p. 70).

Following the trial, Eichmann was found guilty "…of crimes against the Jewish people" and was executed (United States Holocaust Memorial Museum, 2018). Caroline Sharples (2016) argues that Eichmann's trial contributed to a stronger sense of acknowledgement of Germany's responsibility for perpetrating the Holocaust due to "…detailing the deportations to the extermination camps…" and the fact that this trial was "…the first time that the specific plight of the Jews had been at the centre of a war crimes trial" (Sharples, 2016, p. 77). Furthermore, Hannah Arendt's reporting on the Eichmann Trial created fierce controversy over her infamous perspective on "the banality of evil" (Benhabib, 1996, p. 36). Seyla Benhabib (1996) argues that the controversy that ensued from Arendt's *Eichmann in Jerusalem* also sparked further conversations on how to remember victims of the Holocaust:

> Arendt had written about totalitarianism, anti-Semitism, the extermination camps, the Nazi death machinery before. What was unprecedented in the Eichmann affair was that for the first time a struggle broke out...over how and in what terms to appropriate the memory of the Holocaust and its victims (Behabib, 1996, p. 36).

Not only did these effects of the trial further indicate a stronger connection to *Vergangenheitsbewältigung*, but it has also demonstrated an important shift in West German attitudes towards the past overall, especially regarding the Holocaust.

4.6 The '68ers' and *Vergangenheitsbewältigung*

During the 1960s, the ongoing struggle to work through the Nazi past once again came to the forefront of West German society. Youth counter-cultural movements and student-led protests, like those experienced in the United States and abroad at this time, swept through West Germany. However, the youth-led movement in West Germany sparked an unprecedented confrontation of the Nazi past and the Holocaust.

The student movement was highly critical of domestic West German politics, which at this time still contained allegedly denazified individuals who previously served in positions within the Nazi regime. Michael Schmidtke (1999) argues that the primary desire of the protest movement was to spark a change in the West German political system, which they viewed as anti-democratic:

> The main cause of the student protest was a change within the political system...Consequently, by the mid 1960s there existed a German Constitution that declared democracy, but a political culture that repressed democratic values, making it nearly impossible to articulate opposition views outside of the two dominant political parties. Then...the two parties established the Great Coalition which increased political and social opposition and resulted in emerging radical organizations becoming more influential in society and on campuses (Schmidtke, 1999, pp. 78-80)

The perceived inability for West Germany to implement an effective democracy in the eyes of the younger generation ultimately drove protestors to take to the streets nationwide. More importantly, the protests sparked significant intergenerational conflict, with the younger generation of West Germans bringing the Holocaust and Nazism into the forefront of their confrontations with the older generation that had survived World War II. Richard Merritt (1969) argues that this intergenerational conflict was crucial for the next generation of West Germans to begin to build upon previous efforts in confronting their nation's past:

> The generation gap is nonetheless crucial in explaining the particular character of German student unrest. What gives it a special importance is the revulsion felt by many young Germans toward the sins of Nazism. That the generations of their fathers and grandfathers not only permitted Hitler to seize power but also acquiesced in the atrocities committed by Nazism is at best perplexing (Merritt, 1969, p.528).

Questioning their parents' roles during World War II was undoubtedly a critical step forward for all West Germans in confronting their nation's Nazi past. As previously discussed, any dialogue about the Holocaust and the role of Germany in its perpetration was limited and highly controversial in the immediate postwar years. Now, the younger generation of '68ers,' effectively shattered the silence of their parents by confronting and questioning them about their roles and experiences during World War II and the Holocaust. Hans Kundnani (2011) argues that these intergenerational confrontations relative to the Holocaust were a catalyst that created a further shift in West German collective memory of the Nazi past:

> The so-called 1968 generation has often been associated primarily with collective memories in which Germans are perpetrators rather than victims. In particular...the 1968 generation played a key role in the shift in the 1960s from a dominant collective memory centred on Germans as victims to one centered on Germans as perpetrators, in particular by prompting Germany to engage with the Nazi past and in particular the Holocaust (Kundnani, 2011, p. 274).

It is certainly apparent that one of the primary effects of the '68ers' and their movement was a heightened attention towards of the Holocaust and Nazi Germany's role in perpetrating the genocide. Additionally, their movement also highlighted postwar West Germany's failure to fully eradicate the Nazi past, which had proven to be a strong motivator for the 68ers to confront and hold their parents' generation accountable, in their view, as complicit perpetrators rather than victims of fascism. Although smaller movements had slowly advanced the collective notion of *Vergangenheitsbewältigung*, it was the larger protests by the 68ers that truly shattered the victimhood narrative and began to reshape the perspective in which West Germans viewed and remembered the Holocaust as perpetrators.

4.7 The Media: Effects of NBC's *Holocaust* on *Vergangenheitsbewältigung*

The role of the media was also a major factor that brought important and difficult conversations about the Holocaust to the forefront of West German society. It also ushered in a new sense of urgency in confronting the Nazi past, further heightening the importance of *Vergangenheitsbewältigung*. Caroline Sharples (2016) supports this argument and asserts that the media played a crucial role in disseminating accurate representations of the horrors of the Holocaust to ordinary West Germans:

> Information on the Nazi era was steadily reaching bigger audiences, extending into people's own homes…broadcasts, as well as related feature films being screened in…West German cinemas, ensured that the past was becoming more accessible than ever before (Sharples, 2016, p. 127).

Feature films and various broadcasts about the Holocaust certainly aired in West Germany in the years after World War II. However, almost all fell short of accurately portraying murder and genocide. In fact, Caroline Sharples (2016) argues that many films, movies, and documentaries made prior to the late 1970s further peddled the idea that Germans were the victims of fascism by failing to accurately portray the persecution and murder of Jews (Sharples, 2016, p. 129). However, while Sharples' argument is entirely valid, Wulf Kansteiner (2004) argues that the media was a critical vessel in heightening the exposure to the horrors of the Holocaust among West Germans:

> ...television played a crucial role in the process of coming to terms with the nazi past, because the medium relayed to a larger national audience the interpretations of nazism that were originally developed by historians, writers and journalists in Germany and abroad. In this process, scriptwriters, directors and TV administrators served as conduits between the intellectual élite, to which they belong by training and social origin, and the mainstream national public, which they serve (Kansteiner, 2004, p. 576).

Kansteiner's argument accurately highlights the important role that the West German media played in the advancement of *Vergangenheitsbewältigung*. However, no single media program would prove to be more transformational than NBC's *Holocaust* miniseries.

In 1978, NBC first debuted the miniseries *Holocaust* in the United States. By 1979, it was broadcast to West German audiences, where over half of the entire television audience tuned in (Cory, 1980, p. 444). Caroline Sharples (2016) argues that the content portrayed in *Holocaust* truly changed the attitudes and understanding of viewers:

> The series...followed the lives of two families during the Third Reich...it traced the impact of the Nuremberg Laws, Kristallnacht, the 'euthanasia' programme, deportation, ghettoization and, ultimately, the extermination camps...The screening of this series in the FRG has been routinely cited...as constituting a critical turning point in the nation's confrontation with the Nazi past (Sharples, 2016, p. 134).

This emotional and raw depiction of the Holocaust, coupled with the extremely high viewership had immediate impacts on West Germans, argue Andrei Markovits and Rebecca Hayden (1980):

> The amount of family discussion was verified in a survey sent out a week later…in which 64% of those asked had discussed the show with their families…out of 1,800 people questioned, 73% had a positive response to the show…Its emotional effect was undeniable. 64% found the show deeply upsetting, 41% said the show was an important experience for them personally, 39% felt shame that the Germans had committed such crimes and tolerated them as well, 22% claimed there were scenes in which they almost cried…Once again, it was the 14-19 year olds who were most strongly affected, 69% of whom believed that they had learned new facts about Nazism…Considering its more specific educational effect, 56% found that "Holocaust" made certain proceedings during the Nazi period more understandable, 67% thought the show provided a good history lesson for those who did not live at the time, and 49% thought the program should be shown in all schools of the FRG (Markovits & Hayden, 1980, pp. 63, 65-66).

While these survey responses indicated both a transformational and overwhelming response to *Holocaust* by West German audiences, the results also provided strong quantitative evidence that the mini-series was also sparking important conversations about the Holocaust among the public, including claims of responsibility and guilt:

> In discussions with family and friends, the topics most frequently raised were: 1. Film as a whole - 53% with family, 59% with friends, 2. particular scenes - 48% with family, 38% with friends, 3. Causes, question of guilt - 48% with family, 51% with friends… (Markovits & Hayden, 1980, p. 65).

The responses to the surveys conducted after the airing of the mini-series also convey that most respondents felt the need to discuss responsibility and guilt for the perpetration of the Holocaust, which was almost unimaginable just a few years prior. Furthermore, in response to the heightened interest and attention to the Holocaust that resulted from the broadcast, visitor attendance at Dachau rose by about sixty percent compared to before the series aired (Cory, 1980, pp. 444-445). Mark Cory (1980) also argues that a significant effect following the broadcast of *Holocaust,* occurred when the West German government formally abolished the statute of limitations on war crimes, a significant step in ensuring that any pursuit of justice for the horrors committed during the Holocaust could continue (Cory, 1980, pp. 444-445). Never before had West Germany and its citizens reckoned so deeply with guilt and responsibility for the Holocaust to the level witnessed after the broadcast of NBC's *Holocaust*. This was a paramount moment that truly sparked unprecedented Holocaust awareness and memorialization in the coming decades.

4.8 Holocaust Memory Through Counter-Memorials

West Germany's Holocaust memorialization efforts began to increase dramatically during the 1980s and 1990s. While historical sites associated with the Holocaust began to be preserved and protected well before this time, overall memorialization was still nowhere near what can be seen today. Staying true to the prior historical patterns, subsequent generations continued to build on the work of their preceding generation. Historian Brian Ladd (1997) argues that the continuation of the intergenerational pattern led to new memorialization efforts for various groups of victims in Berlin:

> By the 1970s and 1980s, resisters and victims were widely honored, but some younger West Germans were arguing that they had come to serve as the nation's alibi - that Germany had to face up to its identity as the land of Nazis, not anti-Nazis. Why, they asked, do the places of the perpetrators remain unmarked and unacknowledged?...That began to change during the final years of West Berlin, indirectly at first, as the places of the perpetrators were dedicated to honor their victims" (Ladd, 1997, pp. 152-153).

Ladd's (1997) analysis provides further evidence of the ever-changing perspective in which West Germans viewed Holocaust responsibility. It also demonstrates another major advancement of *Vergangenheitsbewältigung* in West German society, through evidence of increased memorialization efforts. While further efforts to erect monuments to victims of the Holocaust would come in the years after reunification, it is first necessary to discuss the counter-monument movement of the 1980s and its effect in spurring further efforts. Noam Lupu (2003) defines counter-monuments as, "…memorial spaces conceived to challenge the very premise of the monument – to be ephemeral rather than permanent, to deconstruct rather than displace memory, to be antiredemptive" (Lupu, 2003, p. 131).

According to Caroline Sharples (2016), counter-monument projects began to appear throughout West Germany during the 1980s, and she argues that these monuments were crucial to engaging audiences with their nation's difficult past:

> One effort to resolve both problems of audience engagement and finding a suitable memorial form for representations of the Holocaust came during the 1980s with the development of the 'counter-monument (*Gegen-Denkmal*) in West Germany. These were abstract memorials that challenged conventional memorial forms and demanded an element of audience participation. The designs were fully conscious of the fact that they were being constructed many years after the Holocaust, and used this temporal distance as an integral part of the memorial, encouraging visitors to reflect upon the role of memory and their own relationship to the Nazi past (Sharples, 2016, p. 115).

These memorials were critically important, both in directly engaging audiences and challenging them to think critically about the roles of Germany and the German people during the Holocaust. Noam Lupu (2003) argues that the counter-monument movement was another important catalyst for West Germans again advancing *Vergangenheitsbewältigung* through "…what scholars have termed the memory boom" (Lupu, 2003, p. 130). This is further evidence that *Vergangenheitsbewältigung* was now of great importance to West Germans and was starting to be represented throughout the public sphere through these various memorials. Many examples of counter-monuments can be identified throughout major West German cities in the years leading up to reunification. In her work, Sharples (2016) identifies a couple of the most well-known counter-monuments that she cites as leading examples, including the Harburg Monument Against Fascism and Aschrott Fountain in Kassel.

What made these memorials so effective in shifting West German attitudes away from older narratives, which tended to absolve Germans of guilt by portraying them as victims too? Lupu (2003) argues that audience engagement with counter-monuments, coinciding with the memory boom at the time, forever changed the way in which West Germans viewed their own history:

> During the…1980s, *Denkmal-Arbeit* [memorial activity] began to shift its focus from the broader German experience with fascism toward the experience of the Holocaust…The new generation…turned to artists for new representations of the Nazi past that could disentangle *Denkmal-Arbeit* from the quest for redemption. The aesthetic and political response was the countermemorial project…memorial spaces conceived to challenge the very premise of the monument - to be ephemeral rather than permanent, to deconstruct rather than displace memory, to be antiredemptive. They would reimpose memorial agency and active involvement on the German public (Lupu, 2003, p. 131).

This new style of memorial engagement, coupled with other developments in Holocaust education and awareness during the 1980s, created an environment which elevated *Vergangenheitsbewältigung* to unprecedented levels of importance. This would have a direct impact on the increased memorialization efforts to honor victims in the years following the reunification of Germany.

4.9 Memorialization Following Reunification

Following the reunification of the country, Germany experienced a significant increase in memorialization efforts to both Jewish and non-Jewish victims of the Holocaust, representing the critical importance of *Vergangenheitsbewältigung*. Caroline Sharples (2016) argues that the increase in memorialization efforts truly represented *Vergangenheitsbewältigung's* permanent position within German collective memory:

> Since German reunification...there has been a veritable boom in the construction of memorials to the Nazi past. Some...have been specially commissioned to commemorate the Holocaust, reflecting its place within the nation's historical consciousness. Other existing monuments...have been subject to a redesign and rededication...Such revisions demonstrate the challenges of incorporating formerly distinct East and West patterns of remembrance into a united, German memorial discourse (Sharples, 2016, p. 105).

Martin Winstone (2010), who has compiled one of the most comprehensive historical guides of Holocaust sites throughout Europe, argues that decades of intergenerational conflict culminated in these increased efforts of contemporary Germans to come to terms with the Nazi past:

> ...from the late 1960s, a younger generation of West Germans sought a more honest understanding of the Holocaust and proper commemoration of it, a process which has accelerated since reunification. There are thus few, if any, countries in Europe where there is greater awareness of the Holocaust or such public memorialisation of it (Winstone, 2010, p.77).

Winstone's (2010) argument is undoubtedly accurate, as it reflects the reality that Germany's progress in memorialization has been built upon by each successive generation of Germans who have asked critical questions and sought meaningful ways to recognize the moral guilt of the nation that perpetrated the Holocaust.

Many of Germany's Holocaust memorials and education centers were publicly unveiled around or right after reunification. These including the Gleis 17 deportation memorial in 1991, the Wannsee House in 1992, and the Topography of Terror exhibit in Berlin, which despite being unveiled in 1987, was made permanent in 1992. While significant memorialization occurred in Berlin, there were countless efforts undertaken at this time throughout the country. The German government has also played a significant role in these efforts by allocating dedicated federal funding to Holocaust memorial sites at former concentration camps and death camps (Smith, 2022). Michael Naumann (2000) argues the importance of federal and state, and local funding for making many of these Holocaust memorial sites and memorial initiatives a reality:

> The government spends some DM 115 million a year on the various memorials and sites of remembrance, the federal states and local authorities probably twice as much again. Over the past decade, Germany has spent over DM 1 billion in building, running and maintaining museums concerned with our recent history as well as the memorials in the former concentration camps situated in Germany. This does not include the over DM 20 million annual funding Germany provides for the International Tracing Service in Arolsen, the world's biggest archive of Holocaust documents. These investments...are the result of an organic process of reflection under way in Germany, both about itself as a nation and about its history (Naumann, 2000, pp. 21-22).

This process of reflection perfectly represents the process by which the concept of *Vergangenheitsbewältigung* became central to memorialization efforts in reunified Germany.

Two well-known examples of post-reunification memorial initiatives in Germany have embodied *Vergangenheitsbewältigung* and convey its meaning directly by engaging audiences. Beginning in 1996, German artist Gunter Demnig, whose father fought for Nazi Germany, began to place small, hand-carved bronze stones within the sidewalks of cities. Considered a counter-monument, the stumbling stones, known as *Stolpersteins*, are designed to cause ordinary Germans and non-Germans stop and think of the nation's perpetration of the Holocaust and more importantly, to remember the victims during the course of their daily lives. Kirsten Harjes (2005) argues that the *Stolperstein* memorials convey the power of memory and a connection to victims of the Holocaust in a rather unique way:

> Rather than presenting a ready-made interpretation of German history, this type of memorial aims to make people think...It emphasizes the educational over the commemorative and representative functions of memorials, and it incorporates a view of historical education as dependent upon active, critical engagement with the past...The designers of *Stolperstein* memorials never claim to represent the

nation in the sense of "standing for" Germany, but many of them do suggest that their memorials "stand for" and "speak for" the victims of the Holocaust...The stones are flush with the street surface, shiny, and evoke the idea of "stumbling" by inviting people to stop, read, and talk about the Holocaust (Harjes, 2005, pp. 143-145).

Incredibly, Demnig's *Stolperstein* memorials, which are now found throughout major cities in Germany, began as an illegal action. When authorities ordered they be removed for other construction to begin, the workers disobeyed, refusing to pull the stones out (Smith, 2022). Since then, the number of *Stolperstein* memorials have grown to greater than 90,000 throughout Germany. The *Stolperstein* memorials are not only the largest decentralized Holocaust memorial in the world, but also the largest decentralized memorial on earth (Smith, 2022).

Each *Stolperstein* was placed in its location deliberately to help contemporary and future generations of Germans and non-Germans to remember victims of the Nazis during the Holocaust. This deliberate and methodical placement also is reflective of Germany embracing the importance of *Vergangenheitsbewältigung* through memorialization efforts. Caroline Sharples (2016) argues that the grassroots style of *Stolperstein* conveys a powerful connection between ordinary Germans and their nation's Nazi past:

> The Stumbling Stones project is also notable for the way it inspires memory work at the grassroots of society...It also encourages people to view the deceased as more than just passive objects; focusing on their last 'voluntary residence' rather than the scene of their murder, and fostering reflection on what their lives may have been like before the rise of Nazism (Sharples, 2016, pp. 124-125).

The meaning conveyed by *Stolperstein* is not only uniquely powerful when compared to other examples of Holocaust memorialization but is also highly effective in helping contemporary citizens envision the once flourishing pre-war community of victims that were destroyed by the Nazi regime.

Another incredible aspect of *Stolperstein* is the production process, which is interconnected with both Holocaust remembrance and *Vergangenheitsbewältigung*. Each *Stolperstein* is handcrafted and hand-installed, a process Demnig cites as critically important, since he believes mass-manufacturing the stones would "...feel akin to the mechanized way that the Nazis killed so many millions of people" (Smith, 2022). Furthermore, the ability for *Stolperstein* to elicit these deep and continuous connections between contemporary Germans and the victims of Nazi atrocities ensures that this dark past is never repeated nor forgotten. Of all Holocaust memorials throughout Germany and beyond, the *Stolperstein* have arguably produced some of the most powerful reactions. Their deliberate placement in everyday spaces beckons citizens to stop, think, and confront Germany's Nazi past, all while ensuring that the stories and experiences of victims live on.

One of the most recognized, and controversial Holocaust memorials in Germany is Berlin's Memorial for the Murdered Jews of Europe, which opened to the public in 2005. Similar to other Holocaust memorialization efforts initiated in years past, this memorial sparked important public discourse and debate relative to how to properly work through the Nazi past. During the mid-1990s, Germans began to discuss the lack of a national memorial to victims of the Holocaust. According to Kirsten Harjes (2005), the Bundestag held two major parliamentary debates over a proposed memorial, what its design might look like, and the role government financing and involvement would play, which included the decision to relinquish of 19,000 square meters of public land for the future site (Harjes, 2005, p. 141). Harjes (2005) further argues that it was these years of controversy and debate that seemed to reinforce Germany's legacy as a leader in coming to terms with their own dark history:

> During the thirteen years that it was planned and debated, the Memorial for the Murdered Jews of Europe came to be associated with the unified government's wish to set a signal of integration: the integration of east and west German collective memory, and Germany's peaceful integration into the European Community and its leading role in it. The memorial also became associated with Germany's official commitment to a distinctly democratic form of collective memory, an aspiration shared by many other countries as well (Harjes, 2005, p. 141).

Caroline Sharples (2016), like Harjes (2005), argues that the various dimensions of the debate regarding the memorial's location, design, and meaning were critical to working through the Nazi past:

> Do memorials simply blend, unnoticed, into the ordinary landscape? How many people will stop, deviate from their purpose and pause to contemplate the meaning of a monument? To some extent, Berlin's Memorial to the Murdered Jews of Europe has circumvented one of these problems: its immense scale and prime location near the Brandenburg Gate, Tiergarten and the Reichstag means that it is not easily ignored...James Young, for instance, declared himself in favour of a continual debate over the form and function of a central Holocaust memorial as offering a better act of remembrance in reunified Germany than any eventual monument (Sharples, 2016, pp. 108-111)

Despite all of the debate and criticism throughout the process, it is important to realize that they each served as an integral part of remembering. This becomes even more important when confronting one's own dark past, such as Germany has done with the help of *Vergangenheitsbewältigung*.

The Memorial to the Murdered Jews of Europe was officially dedicated and opened to the public in 2005 after receiving over €25 million in direct government funding approved by the Bundestag. Further approved funding also allowed for the construction of an underground museum and information center beneath the memorial.

Martin Winstone (2010) provides key analysis on the finished memorial's design and how it conveys the meaning of *Vergangenheitsbewältigung*:

> The largest cluster of memorials in Berlin is at the other end of Unter den Linden by the Tiergarten. The most prominent is the Memorial to the Murdered Jews of Europe, a 19,000-square-metre site covered in an undulating field of 2,711 large concrete blocks which rather resembles an enormous Jewish cemetery from afar. Its location in the centre of the city is a clear statement of intent to remember..." (Winstone, 2010, p. 85).

Harjes (2005) similarly argues that the design of the memorial was critically important and meant to convey a deeply emotional impact on individuals and tourists visiting the site:

> Whereas every type or size of memorial is meant to elicit emotions, the experienced-based memorial foregrounds this intention, investing much effort and expense on an elaborate manipulation of reality...The designer of the national Holocaust memorial expects visitors walking among the thousands of narrowly spaced stelae to experience feelings of claustrophobia and oppression reminiscent of the experience of Jews in the concentration camps (Harjes, 2005, p. 142).

The completed memorial's massive size and location within downtown Berlin both represents and further fortifies the centrality of responsibility and memory as part of the process of *Vergangenheitsbewältigung*.

Chapter V - Conclusion

This thesis examines the complex process in which Germany has created and fostered an environment remembering and honoring victims of the Holocaust through memorialization, education, and the embracement of *Vergangenheitsbewältigung*. Immediately after World War II, Germans rarely spoke of the Holocaust or their roles in it. If they did, the narrative most often provided was that Germans were victims of fascism. Additionally, the trauma of forced confrontation by Allied occupiers, coupled with the unprecedented physical destruction of Germany, proved to be motivating factors behind the silence. Despite this reality, the first postwar generation began critically examining and confronting the silence and victimhood narratives of their predecessors. The younger generation began to ask their parents what their roles were, or what they did during the Holocaust, continuing the process in which successive generations embraced *Vergangenheitsbewältigung*. This process reached unprecedented attention with the movement of the 68ers. Their actions created an environment where discussing the Holocaust and Germany's role in its perpetration was not only accepted but encouraged to further work to overcome the Nazi past.

The Cold War dynamic of a divided Germany also had an important effect on the overall memorialization process. Ultimately, it was this dynamic that led an economically ravaged West Germany into reparations negotiations with Israel. Chancellor Konrad Adenauer hoped this would help his nation become reintegrated into the Western world, both politically and economically. Beyond the geopolitical situation of the Cold War, West Germany also established the beginnings of an effective Holocaust educational curriculum in schools, which in turn led to further engagement with the past by younger citizens. This has continued to develop and grow, with Holocaust educational frameworks mandated for German students. The effects of the media and literature on Holocaust awareness and *Vergangenheitsbewältigung* should not be ignored either, as Anne Frank's *The Diary of a Young Girl* and NBC's *Holocaust* miniseries were transformational moments that reenforced the importance of these topics to the identity of German collective memory. As a result of these various factors, Germany witnessed a drastic growth in the total number of memorials, museums, and educational centers dedicated to the history of the Holocaust and to the memory of victims. This process has continued well beyond reunification and has been a major contributor to Germany's global reputation as a nation that has perhaps done more to overcome its own dark past more than any other.

My overall purpose in this thesis was to examine various significant moments and determine the factors that have led to Germany's contemporary reputation as a model of reconciliation and confronting the past. Specifically, my thesis attempts to determine how Germany, a nation of perpetrators, has come to recognize and memorialize their victims, as well as create a culture of remembrance and reconciliation. Research and analysis of existing evidentiary sources certainly indicate that embracing the concept of *Vergangenheitsbewältigung* has driven the process of memorializing victims of the Holocaust in Germany. It has also helped place Holocaust education and memory at the forefront of German collective memory. Strong support from German government has provided unprecedented public funding for monuments, memorials, and other projects that helped to further reinforce the crucial importance of *Vergangenheitsbewältigung*. According to Michael Naumann (2000), there are more than 4,000 publicly funded museums that are used as places of education for current and future generations of Germans to recognize the responsibility their nation holds in perpetrating the Holocaust (Naumann, 2000, p. 21).

While Germany has gained its reputation for effectively working through the difficulties of the Nazi past, it must be noted that this process has been far from perfect. Historian A. Dirk Moses (2021) presents many criticisms of Germany's process of working through the past when compared to other atrocities in what he terms 'The German Catechism':

> In short, the catechism implies a redemptive story in which the sacrifice of Jews in the Holocaust by Nazis is the premise for the Federal Republic's legitimacy. That is why the Holocaust is more than an important historical event. It is a sacred trauma that cannot be contaminated by profane ones – meaning non-Jewish victims and other genocides – that would vitiate its sacrificial function (Moses, 2021).

While often viewed as controversial, his argument raises several points that should be discussed and noted. First, Moses (2021) argues that working through the Nazi past, for the most part, has superseded memory and responsibility for other acts of historical violence by the German Empire. Reinhart Kössler (2012) asserts that this criticism is entirely merited when examining the atrocities committed by the German Empire in Namibia:

> After World War II, colonial revisionism was no more an option, and a clear discursive break occurred. In West Germany, nurturing the tradition of the *Schutztruppe* was relegated to rather marginal groups while a majority found themselves preoccupied with seemingly more pressing issues. Moreover, for those who undertook seriously to grapple with Germany's dire past of the first half of the 20th century, the shadow of the Shoah tended to overwhelm other concerns (Kössler, 2012, p. 282).

While steps have been taken to reconcile with Namibia, including an agreement for reparations, Germany has fallen well short when compared to efforts related to the

Holocaust. Additionally, Germany has also faced other criticisms that reinforce Moses's (2021) argument regarding the new 'German catechism,' including the nation's response to the migrant crisis, the rise in neo-Nazi activity, and the increase in far-right political parties, most notably *Alternative für Deutschland*, or AfD. Diethelm Prowe (1997) argues that the post-Cold War extreme right in Germany has directly contradicted the idea of *Vergangenheitsbewältigung*:

> The radical Right's shrill voices of hatred and the intermittent electoral gains of the rightist parties have left the widespread impression that this post-Cold War extreme right is tantamount to a reawakening Nazism…The lore of the Nazi years has provided a wellspring of inspiration and basic myths for the whole spectrum of today's radical right. Even those neo-conservatives, who condemn Hitler's judeocide, direct their most furious attacks against the eternal shackle of guilt the Holocaust has imposed on German history and identity (Prowe, 1997, p. 1).

Despite these legitimate criticisms, Germany has proven that it has crafted an identity that strongly emphasizes *Vergangenheitsbewältigung*. As such, Germany should be viewed as a leader in working through the difficulties of its past to create a new collective identity, one that recognizes its victims and strives to ensure that no one ever forgets. Germany still has much work to do in confronting its colonial past as well as contemporary issues such as anti-immigration and far-right nationalism. While Germany is internationally recognized and praised for its efforts, further research for the purpose of conducting comparative analyses with other steps taken by post-genocidal nations would be helpful in identifying what specific aspects work to foster a culture of remembrance and which do not.

Literature Cited

Anthon, C. G. (1963). The End of the Adenauer Era. *Current History, 44*(260), 193–201. http://www.jstor.org/stable/45310903

Benhabib, S. (1996). Identity, Perspective and Narrative in Hannah Arendt's "Eichmann in Jerusalem." *History and Memory, 8*(2), 35–59. http://www.jstor.org/stable/25618705

Collins German-English Dictionary. (2023) *Vergangenheitsbewältigung Definition.* https://www.collinsdictionary.com/dictionary/german-english/vergangenheitsbewaltigung

Colls, C. S. (2016). 'Earth conceal not my blood': forensic and archaeological approaches to locating the remains of Holocaust victims. In J.-M. Dreyfus & É. Anstett (Eds.), *Human Remains in Society: Curation and Exhibition in the Aftermath of Genocide and Mass-violence* (pp. 163–196). Manchester University Press. http://www.jstor.org/stable/j.ctt21h4xwg.13

Cory, Mark E. "Some Reflections on NBC's Film Holocaust." *The German Quarterly*, vol. 53, no. 4, 1980, pp. 444–51. *JSTOR*, https://doi.org/10.2307/404545. Accessed 5 Jan. 2023.

Dobel, J. P. (1998). Political Prudence and the Ethics of Leadership. *Public Administration Review, 58*(1), 74–81. https://doi.org/10.2307/976892

Fink, C. (2007). Turning Away from the Past: West Germany and Israel, 1965–1967. In P. Gassert & A. E. Steinweis (Eds.), *Coping With the Nazi Past: West German Debates on Nazism and Generational Conflict, 1955-1975* (1st ed., pp. 276–293). Berghahn Books. http://www.jstor.org/stable/j.ctt9qdg5n.20

Funkenstein, A. (1989). Collective Memory and Historical Consciousness. *History and Memory, 1*(1), 5–26. http://www.jstor.org/stable/25618571

Halbwachs, M. (1992). *On Collective Memory.* University of Chicago Press. p. 53.

Harjes, K. (2005). Stumbling Stones: Holocaust Memorials, National Identity, and Democratic Inclusion in Berlin. *German Politics & Society, 23*(1 (74)), 138–151. http://www.jstor.org/stable/23740916

Holocaust misconceptions. Illinois Holocaust Museum & Education Center. (2023). Retrieved January 27, 2023, from https://www.ilholocaustmuseum.org/holocaust-misconceptions/

Janowitz, M. (1946). German Reactions to Nazi Atrocities. *American Journal of Sociology, 52*(2), 141–146. http://www.jstor.org/stable/2770938

Kansteiner, W. (1999). Mandarins in the Public Sphere: Vergangenheitsbewältigung and the Paradigm of Social History in the Federal Republic of Germany. *German Politics & Society, 17*(3 (52)), 84–120. http://www.jstor.org/stable/23737394

Kansteiner, W. (2004). Nazis, Viewers and Statistics: Television History, Television Audience Research and Collective Memory in West Germany. *Journal of Contemporary History, 39*(4), 575–598. http://www.jstor.org/stable/4141411

Kössler, R. (2012). Facing Postcolonial Entanglement and the Challenge of Responsibility: Actor Constellations between Namibia and Germany. In B. Schwelling (Ed.), *Reconciliation, Civil Society, and the Politics of Memory: Transnational Initiatives in the 20th and 21st Century* (pp. 277–312). Transcript Verlag. http://www.jstor.org/stable/j.ctv1xxswv.12

Kundnani, H. (2011). Perpetrators and Victims: Germany's 1968 Generation and Collective Memory. *German Life & Letters, 64*(2), 272-282. https://doi-org.umasslowell.idm.oclc.org/10.1111/j.1468-0483.2010.01533.x

Ladd, B. (1997). *The Ghosts of Berlin: Confronting German History in the Urban Landscape.* The University of Chicago Press. pp. 152-153.

Lupu, N. (2003). Memory Vanished, Absent, and Confined: *The Countermemorial Project in 1980s and 1990s Germany. History and Memory, 15*(2), 130–164. https://doi.org/10.2979/his.2003.15.2.130

Marcuse, H. (1998). The Revival of Holocaust Awareness in West Germany, Israel, and the United States. In: C. Fink et al., *1968: The World Transformed* (pp. 421-439). The German Historical Institute.

Markovits, A. S., & Hayden, R. S. (1980). "Holocaust" before and after the Event: Reactions in West Germany and Austria. *New German Critique, 19*, 53–80. https://doi.org/10.2307/487972

Mauriello, C. (2017). *Forced Confrontation: The Politics of Dead Bodies in Germany at the End of World War II*. Lexington Books. pp. 181-182.

Merriam-Webster. (2023). *Memory Definition*. https://www.merriam-webster.com/dictionary/memory

Merriam-Webster. (2023). *Responsibility Definition*. https://www.merriam-webster.com/dictionary/responsibility

Merriam-Webster.. (2023). *Memorialize Definition*. https://www.merriam-webster.com/dictionary/memorialize

Merritt, R. L. (1969). The Student Protest Movement in West Berlin. *Comparative Politics, 1*(4), 516–533. https://doi.org/10.2307/421493

Moses, A. D. (2007). The Non-German German and the German German: Dilemmas of Identity after the Holocaust. *New German Critique, 101*, 45–94. http://www.jstor.org/stable/27669198

Moses, A. D. (2021, May 23). *The German Catechism*. Geschichte der Gegenwart. Retrieved December 29, 2022, from https://geschichtedergegenwart.ch/the-german-catechism/

Naumann, M. (2000). Remembrance and Political Reality: Historical Consciousness in Germany after the Genocide. *New German Critique, 80*, 17–28. https://doi.org/10.2307/488630

Olick, J. K., & Levy, D. (1997). Collective Memory and Cultural Constraint: Holocaust Myth and Rationality in German Politics. *American Sociological Review, 62*(6), 921–936. https://doi.org/10.2307/2657347

Olick, J.K. (2003). The guilt of nations? *Ethics & International Affairs, 17(2)*, 109+. https://link.gale.com/apps/doc/A139107200/EAIM?u=mlin_n_umass&sid=bookmark-EAIM&xid=79862b22

Pagaard, S. A. (1995). German Schools and the Holocaust: A Focus on the Secondary School System of Nordrhein-Westfalen. *The History Teacher, 28*(4), 541–554. https://doi.org/10.2307/494641

Prowe, D. (1997). National Identity and Racial Nationalism in the New Germany: Nazism versus the Contemporary Radical Right. *German Politics & Society, 15*(1 (42)), 1–21. http://www.jstor.org/stable/23736533

Rees, L. (2017). *The Holocaust: A New History*. PublicAffairs. p. 12.

Rothberg, M. (2009). *Multidirectional Memory: Remembering the Holocaust in the Age of Decolonialization*. Stanford University Press. pp. 6-7.

Sagan, A. (1995). An Optimistic Icon: Anne Frank's Canonization in Postwar Culture. *German Politics & Society, 13*(3 (36)), 95–107. http://www.jstor.org/stable/23736492

Schmidtke, M. A. (1999). Cultural Revolution or Cultural Shock? Student Radicalism and 1968 in Germany. *South Central Review, 16/17*, 77–89. https://doi.org/10.2307/3190078

Sharples, C. (2016). *Postwar Germany and the Holocaust*. Bloomsbury Academic. pp. 57-150.

Smith, C. (2022, November 14). *Monuments to the Unthinkable*. The Atlantic. Retrieved January 17, 2023, from https://www.theatlantic.com/magazine/archive/2022/12/holocaust-remembrance-lessons-america/671893/

United States Holocaust Memorial Museum. "Adolf Eichmann." Holocaust
    Encyclopedia. https://encyclopedia.ushmm.org/content/en/article/adolf-eichmann

Winstone, M. (2010). *The Holocaust Sites of Europe*. I.B. Taurus. pp. 77-85.

Appendix

Visual examples of Holocaust memorials and education centers throughout Germany

All Photographs Courtesy of Nolan King

Figure 1 – *Stolperstein* for Ella & Meta Thorner in Berlin

Figure 2 – Two examples of *Stolperstein* in a Berlin sidewalk

Figure 3 – View of the Memorial to the Murdered Jews of Europe in Berlin

Figure 4 – Undulating *stelae* of the Memorial to the Murdered Jews of Europe in Berlin

Figure 5 – More undulating *stelae* of the Memorial to the Murdered Jews of Europe

Figure 6 – View from within the Memorial to the Murdered Jews of Europe

Figure 7 – Entrance to the Memorial to the Sinti and Roma Victims of National Socialism in the Tiergarten, Berlin

Figure 8 – The Memorial to the Sinti and Roma Victims of National Socialism

Figure 9 – View of the Topography of Terror exhibit in Berlin

Figure 10 – Part of exhibit at the Topography of Terror in Berlin

Figure 11 – Platform 17 Memorial at Berlin-Grunewald Station

Figure 12 – Iron plate at Platform 17 indicating the deportation of 1,000 Jews from Berlin to Theresienstadt on September 14, 1942.

Figure 13 – Iron plates indicating the deportation of Jews from Berlin to Auschwitz and Theresienstadt. Each plate indicates the date, destination, and total number for each series of deportations that occurred here.

Figure 14 – Memorial to the Deported Jews in Berlin next to the entrance to the Platform 17 Memorial in Berlin.

Figure 15 – Exterior of the House of the Wannsee Conference in Berlin. The house is now a memorial museum and educational site

Figure 16 – Memorial stone in Regensburg, Germany. The memorial is dedicated to the victims of the Regensburg subcamp of Flossenbürg Concentration Camp

Figure 17 – Example of exhibit at the Nazi Party Rally Grounds Documentation Center in Nuremberg, Germany

www.ingramcontent.com/pod-product-compliance
Lightning Source LLC
Chambersburg PA
CBHW071843290426
44109CB00017B/1913